GERMAN MOTORCYCLES IN WORLD WAR II

BMW, DKW, NSU, TRIUMPH, VIKTORIA, ZÜNDAPP

by
STEFAN KNITTEL

Left page: Motorcycle riflemen with their Zündapp K 500 cycles at a maneuver-type Wehrmacht show in Hainberg, 1937.

Schiffer Publishing Ltd®

4880 Lower Valley Road, Atglen, Pennsylvania 19310

PHOTO SOURCES:

Federal Archives, Cologne (BA)
Archives of the Bayerische Motoren-Werke AG, Munich
Archives of the Zündapp-Werke GmbH, Munich
Scheibert Archives
Motorbureau Archives

The author would like to express thanks for their friendly support to Dr. Trumpp of the Federal Archives, Mr. Fleischmann of BMW, Mr. Kletzke of Zündapp, Mr. Schneider of the Auto & Technik Museum in Sinsheim, Mr. Karl-Heinz Denzler, Mr. Dieter Lehner, Mr. Hermann Schimkat, Mr. Karl Reese and Mr. Peter Miller.

Translated from the German by Dr. Edward Force.

Library of Congress Catalog Number: 89-063359.

ISBN: 978-0-88470-205-0
Printed in China.

Published by Schiffer Publishing Ltd.
4880 Lower Valley Road
Atglen, PA 19310
Phone: (610) 593-1777;
Fax: (610) 593-2002
E-mail: Info@schifferbooks.com

In Europe, Schiffer books are distributed by
Bushwood Books
6 Marksbury Ave.
Kew Gardens
Surrey TW9 4JF England
Phone: 44 (0) 20 8392-8585;
Fax: 44 (0) 20 8392-9876
E-mail: info@bushwoodbooks.co.uk
Website: www.bushwoodbooks.co.uk

The Motorcycles in the German Army

Around the turn of the century, motorization, still in its infancy, made a great advance, but the military leadership, being rather conservative, took no notice of this development at first. The horse was still seen as its main means of mobility and transport. Thus the use of eleven Neckarsulm (NSU) motorcycles at the Imperial Maneuvers of 1904 came as a great surprise. The value of the motorcycle as a courier's vehicle was clear to see, and when, as of about 1911, powerful machines with attached sidecars were available, someone got the idea of creating a mobile machine-gun emplacement. This was not destined to prove itself, though, in the rigorous operations of World War I. But all the same, 5400 motorcycles were used in the Imperial Army from 1914 to 1918, most of them V-2 machines built by the firms of NSU and Wanderer, which gave good service as relatively fast courier vehicles (in comparison to the automobiles that were still very troublesome then).

In the Twenties the motorcycle gradually established itself in a broad spectrum of official uses, at first in the police and then in the postal and customs systems and other departments as well. At that time too the expression "Krad" was introduced as a short form of the official designation of "Kraftrad". The sidecar arrangement, as a speedy vehicle that was, moreover, much more economical than the automobile, was included in the reorganization of the Reichswehr from 1927 on and given a new job. In addition to being used by communication, transport and recon-

The typical motorcyclist's equipment was represented by the motorcycle messenger's coat. It could be buttoned around the legs, rather like trousers, and thus offered good protection from wind and weather.

A motorcycle rifle column moves out. The marching order created endlessly long columns of motorcycle riders, whom it was often difficult to command.

Here a repair company in Russia has set up an improvised field workshop. The "sporting spirit" among the motorcyclists is documented by the sign.

naissance units, its potential for tactical operations was recognized. Motorcycle rifle companies were established, some with three armed soldiers aboard, others with a machine gun mounted on the sidecar, which were seen as very mobile attack units, similar to the earlier cavalry.

In choosing machines, proven types from the native motorcycle industry's civilian production programs were selected. From the Victoria-Werke of Nürnberg the KR VI, with its longitudinally opposed 600 cc motor, was chosen, and from BMW of Munich at first the 750 cc Types R 62 and R 11. These orders, limited to a few thousand motorcycles in all, were the first official contracts for BMW, a small business that was soon to gain great importance, which it has maintained to this day, as is well known. The first big procurement program extended into 1932 with the single-cylinder BMW R 4, which was introduced as the standard training machine.

As of 1933-34 the motorcycle rifle companies were integrated into the reconnaissance units, and the organization of whole motorcycle rifle battalions was planned. For this reason, large orders were given to the manufacturers. Along with BMW, Zündapp of Nürnberg also received a big order. To the two-cylinder, 500 or 750 cc machines there were attached sidecars of a standard type, the so-called "official boat", saddlebag racks were mounted, cross-country tires were put on, and the vehicles were painted field gray. No other technical changes were made, for the motorcycles, most of which were in series production, were considered to be thoroughly suited to military use. In contrast, expensive special car and truck types were required, as is well known.

Universal conscription was restored in Germany in 1935, which gave the signal to start equipping the army, now called the "Wehrmacht". The infantry and artillery were now accompanied by the new and very promising armored troops, and the motorcycle riflemen were likewise regarded as a separate class of weapons, which could complement the more ponderous armored units with their speed and mobility. The requirements for a troop with almost universal operational possibilities depended most of all, of course, on the quality of their training. As a result, the motorcycle rifle battalion soldiers were given extensive weapons and combat training, as well as engineering training and, above all, thorough motorcycle training. In addition to complete technical and maintenance training, driver training in itself was valued most highly. Here the recruits were introduced to the "high school of motorcycle driving", with stringent drill and thorough practice programs (driving on sand, hard and soft ground, steep slopes, through or over ditches and straight through forests and fields). The soldiers could put their ability to the test in many driving contests within the army, as well as in civilian sports events.

An army workshop in which both repair work and the reequipping of requisitioned civilian motorcycles are carried on.

The repair troop, present in every motorcycle rifle company, provided fast service underway and in the field.

The two soldiers are using a requisitioned machine, but this time not a civilian cycle but a captured English machine (Norton 500).

In 1938, preparations for war were shifted into high gear; solo courier cycles were ordered in great numbers from BMW, DKW, NSU, Triumph, Victoria and Zündapp, and naturally the number of sidecar units was also increased considerably. When the war began with the march into Poland in September of 1939, the motorcycle riders were able to fulfill their assigned tasks splendidly, just as they did in the French campaign shortly thereafter. But as the war's activities spread out over the Balkans to North Africa, and particularly with the attack on the Soviet Union, the difficulties began. While until now a relatively good network of roads and cultivated (in two senses) terrain had been found, the advance routes to Russia, especially during outbreaks of bad weather, soon created barriers that the motorcycles, with their limited cross-country capability, could not overcome. Losses increased drastically, and more and more privately owned motorcycles were commandeered for Wehrmacht use, which brought on another problem, namely the necessity of maintaining much greater stores of spare parts. Even before that there had been no uniformity of motorcycles in the various categories, so that the confusion now became all the greater.

In the summer of 1941, when the first examples of the heavy cross-country units conceived especially for military use, comprising a BMW R 75 or Zündapp KS 750 and a powered sidecar, reached the front, most of the original motorcycle rifle units had already been attached to other groups. As of 1942 the whole concept of motorcycle riflemen had been given up, and the motorcycle units had been attached to the reconnaissance battalions. The motorcycle messengers and couriers, like all other motorcycle drivers in the Wehrmacht, were meanwhile excited about the new vehicles, which made advancing possible under even the worst conditions. At about the same time, the VW "bucket car" and VW amphibian were introduced, vehicles that had actually been seen as replacements for the unsatisfactory motorcycles of the first era of motorcycle rifle unit development. Naturally, these vehicles could not replace a motorcycle, but their production costs were only half as high as those of the unbelievably expensive cross-country units, and so they were given priority. But by this time some 35,000 of these units had been built, for in terms of maneuverability and handling in heavy country, they ranked remarkably above all competition throughout the whole war.

Even though the commotion about the "fast troops", the "motorcycle hussars", that the propaganda people had created, had died down quickly in the war, the motorcycle riders still accomplished something remarkable. They were much faster and more mobile than their comrades, they could get their defective cycles going again quickly in most cases, and were often very attached to their machines, for they knew what degree of reliability they could attain through their own service and maintenance-as long as they had the chance. On the other hand, there was the grim reality of a constantly worsening situation as regarded supplies of spare parts and fuel, as well as, naturally, the

questionable suitability of so many products for war use. As in all other areas of the Wehrmacht, all planning and conception for the motorcycle units were overwhelmed by the grim reality of the war.

Right page:
Left: A messenger rider in Florence in 1944. His motorcycle, the BMW R 4, was used by the army from 2932 to 1936 and seems to have lasted a long time. (BA)
Right: A propaganda photo from the Polish campaign in 1939, in which two motorcycle riflemen in regulation dress lift a requisitioned civilian machine, a BMW R 23 (250 cc), over a brook. The motorcycle was equipped with neither a headlight cover nor the uniform saddlebags. (BA)

BMW

Probably the most famous German motorcycle firm, located in Munich, has been the main supplier of official motorcycles from the Twenties to the present. The first orders from military authorities came in 1927. But the one-cylinder R 4 (400 cc) was the first cycle to be delivered in large numbers, beginning in 1932; this extremely robust model also served as a messenger's vehicle at first, though most of them were used in the training companies. In 1937 the modernized R 35 took their place, and was supplied until 1940. These two ponderous one-cylinder BMW's were not very popular among the troops, which may have been brought on by the men's unpleasant memories of the strict training programs of their recruit days. In the realm of heavy military motorcycles, BMW had a strong competitor for military contracts in the Zündapp firm of Nürnberg; both used the same construction concepts, with a transverse two-cylinder opposed motor in a pressed-steel frame. With the side-valve 750 cc Type R 12, available from 1935 on, the Munich firm had made a good move. This machine, with only 18 horsepower, could offer a remarkably reliable powerplant and was very well suited to the heavy sidecar unit. The Wehrmacht's test centers were immediately convinced of the BMW R 12's quality, and this resulted in the largest single order for military motorcycles; as of May 1941, BMW had delivered no fewer than 36,000 R 12 machines to the Wehrmacht. As an important supplier, BMW was also involved in the construction contract for a special military cross-country motorcycle. But because the requirements varied considerably on account of the different operational uses, the beginning of production was postponed several times. Only in June of 1941 could the first R 75 leave the factory; a year later production was transferred from Munich to Eisenach, as the main factory was concentrating on aircraft motors. Of the costly R 75 with powered sidecar, differential, cross-country and reverse gears, plus hydraulic brakes on the rear wheel and sidecar, some 17,000 were built by the autumn of 1944. The sidecars were a group project of the three leading manufacturers, Steib, Stoye and Royal.

Left: The BMW R 35 medium Wehrmacht motorcycle. The 350 cc BMW with its telescopic fork without shock absorbers replaced the R 4 in 1937; it was used in great numbers in the training of Wehrmacht motorcyclists.

Lower left: A Wehrmacht column changes its position within Germany. The leading unit is a requisitioned civilian vehicle, a BMW R 61 with a Steib sports sidecar. (BA)

Below: This BMW R 12 in service with the field police comes from the first Wehrmacht delivery of 1935. The gigantic front fender was soon given up, for it filled up too easily with dirt. (BA)

Right: A press photo from France in 1940. Here again we see a requisitioned civilian vehicle; at the left in the photo is a BMW R 51, while the unit in the center is a BMW R 61 with a Steib sidecar. (BA)

Lower right: A BMW R 61 that was certainly not among those ordered by the Wehrmacht, but of which several hundred examples were delivered to government agencies. Here we see a vehicle of the field police in the 5th Mountain Division.

Below: The BMW R 4 was the oldest motorcycle in military service when the war began; it had been introduced by the Reichswehr as of 1932 and used mainly for the training of recruits. The robust 12-HP 400 cc motor and the stable pressed-steel leaf-spring fork made this machine an extremely reliable vehicle for demanding courier service. The military version differed from the civilian model, aside from its paint, only in its saddlebag brackets and the motor-protecting plate on the lower frame.

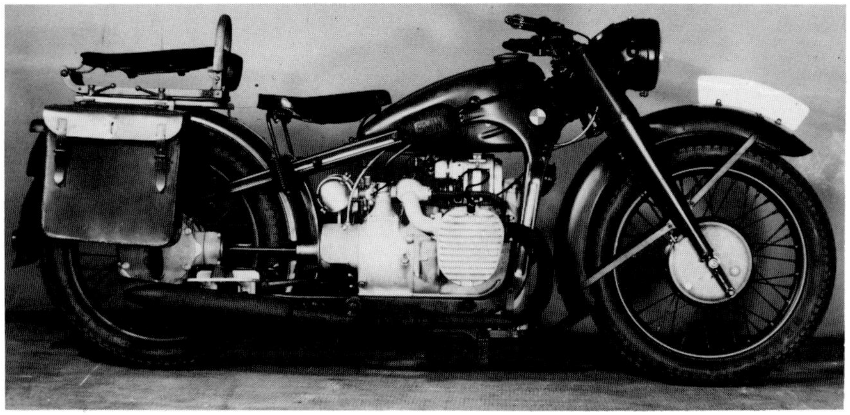

Left: the most frequently used heavy Wehrmacht motorcycle, the 745 cc BMW R 12, which was used in both solo and sidecar versions. The picture shows the modified official version, which has footrests instead of aluminum footboards, plus a shoe-sole protector on the exhaust pipe. The sheet-metal fenders were also flatter. The R 12 was very popular on account of its sturdiness, but it had only limited cross-country use.

Opposite page:
Right: The BMW R 12 as introduced into the army in 1935, when the first machines were put into service with footboards and large fenders.

Below: The R 12 with the uniform official sidecar; along with the Zündapp models, these were the standard equipment of the motorcycle riflemen. This unit was supplied until May of 1941.

Below: A column of the 12th Armored Division advancing through Russia in the summer of 1941. The BMW R 12 drivers make the most of a pause.

Bottom: A motorcycle rifle unit in training (all on BMW R 12) before the French campaign of 1940. (BA)

Lower right: 50 BMW R 12 sidecar units and several solo machines at the Munich factory, ready for delivery to the Wehrmacht. (BA)

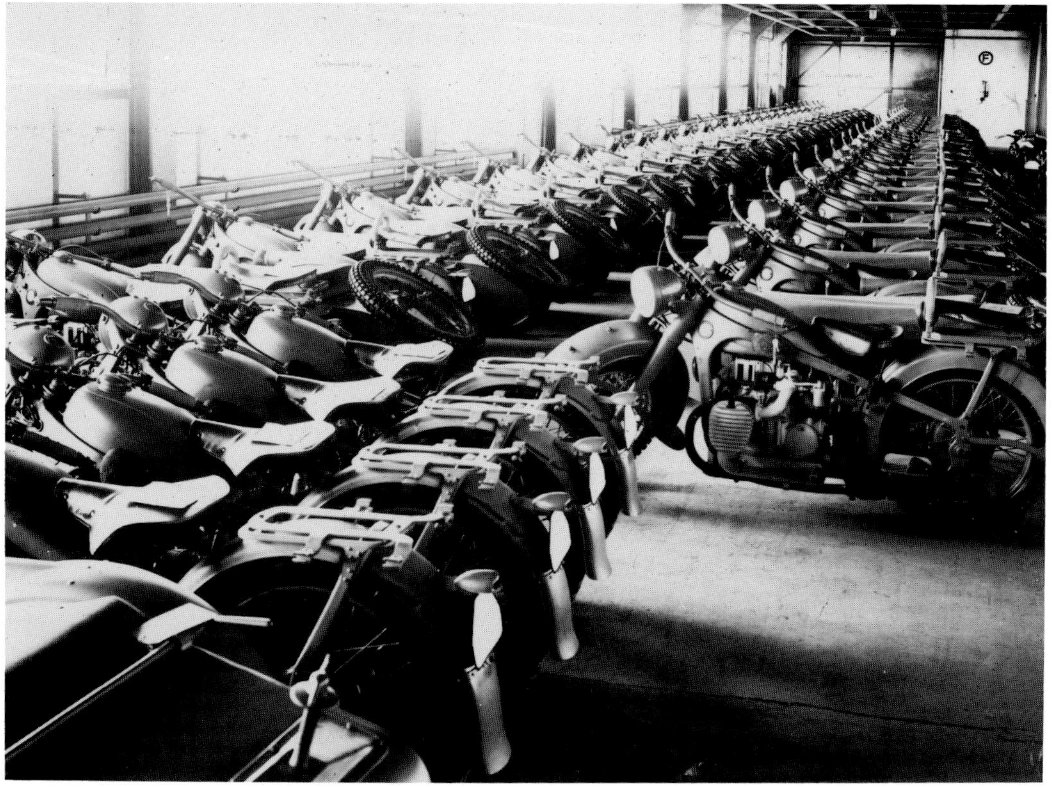

Left: Start-mount! BMW 12's in the West during the Winter of 1940. (BA)

Lower left: A BMW R 12 being serviced. The Berlin registration suggests a requisitioned machine that has been partially adapted to Wehrmacht standards (fender brace, paint). (BA)

Below: Prescribed mastering of a ditch with the sidecar unit, a practice session in 1940, again using a BMW R 12. (BA)

Opposite page:
Above: The fast troop in Paris, a group of messenger riders with their R 12 solo machines. (BA)

Below: Greece in April of 1941-the motorcycle riflemen on their R 12's roll over a corduroy road. (BA)

Bottom: The motorcycle riflemen with their R 12 sidecar units appear in 1940 propaganda pictures. (BA)
Far right: Motorcycle riflemen of the SS Division "Leibstandarte Adolf Hitler" (LAH) in Russia. (BA)

WH
199 119

Partisanen-Gefahr
von Welish
halt!
Durchfahrt
aufwärts
Waffen
Der Kommand.
General.
Pol
1230
WH

PK
WH-408832
K

Opposite page:
Upper left: Two R 12 sidecar units meet at the entrance to a depot in northern Russia in the autumn of 1941. (BA)

Upper right: A field police sentry at Witebsk in 1941. The sidecar on the R 12 is a civilian model. (BA)

Below: A typical picture from Russia; the heavy sidecar units get stuck in the mud all too easily, as has the R 12 of a propaganda company here. (BA)

This page:
Left: Motorcycles during a troop relocation by railroad, with an R 12 in the foreground and the new BMW R 75 behind it. (BA)

Lower left: The Russian winter: the 18-horsepower R 12 is towed by one horsepower. (BA)

Below: The motorcycle riflemen of the Guderian armored group have taken cover, as the mounted MG 34 made the sidecar units a good offensive weapon, but under enemy fire the crew was unprotected. (BA)

Left: Three R 12 sidecar units of the Afrika-Korps in a sandstorm. With appropriate service, especially to the air filter, these vehicles also gave reliable service in the desert. (BA)

Lower left: Motorcycle riflemen in Russia in March of 1943, on the march. (BA)

Below: The motorcycle messenger looks friendly, but one can imagine the hardships he has been through by noting the condition of his R 12.

Left: The overweight BMW R 75 Wehrmacht sidecar unit, the development of which was taken up only after the war began and oriented to changed operational conditions. In the latter half of 1941 the first vehicles were delivered to the troops.

Below: The R 75 without its sidecar. The greatest innovation in this machine was the additional drive for the sidecar wheel via a differential, with wheel-pressure dependent torque equalization. The gearbox included both a cross-country and a reverse gear.

Left: In the planning of the R 75, emphasis was placed on an organic unity of cycle and sidecar. Despite the heavy weight of more than 400 kilograms, the units proved to be extremely handy and suited to cross-country driving.

Below: The R 75 unit seen from the motorcycle side, here a modified 1942-43 version with rubber cylinders on the front fork, the high-mounted air filter on the tank, and the leg protectors over the cylinders; the fenders have also been made flatter. The rear tire visible in this photo could scarcely have met with the approval of the troops . . .

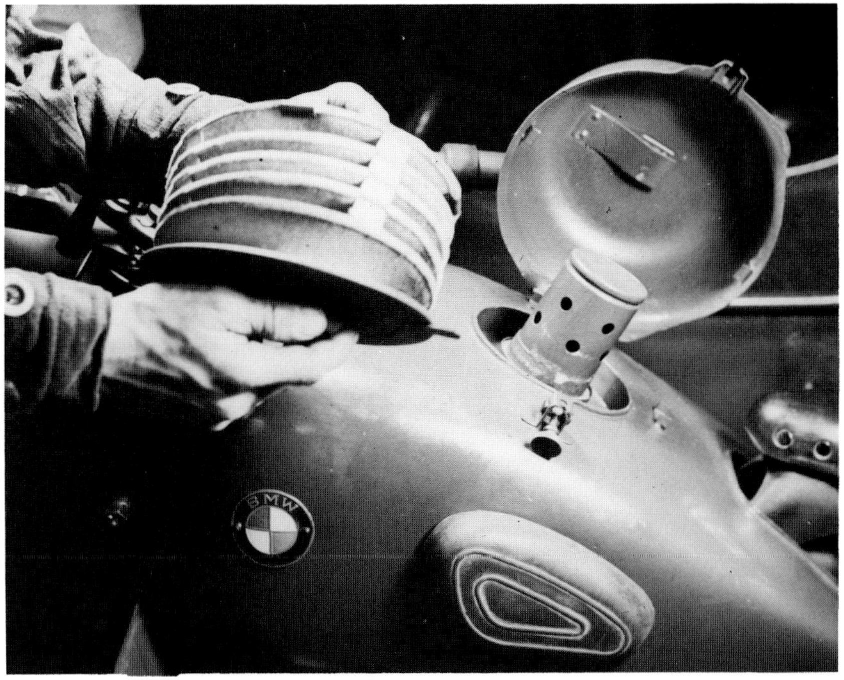

Left: Here the so-called tropical filter of the R 75 can be seen in detail. The filter, originally mounted on the engine block, became clogged much too quickly, forcing this modification.

Lower left: The newly built 750 cc overhead valve motor of the R 75; its performance, kept at the relatively low level of 26 HP, was one reason for its legendary reliability.

Below: Final preparation of the R 75 at the BMW factory; the BW 43 uniform sidecar is being attached.

Left: A motorcycle rifle company of the "Hermann Göring" (HG) Armored Division on German territory early in 1942, obviously just equipped with the new R 75 units. The heavy loads did not matter to these big units, as the very first plans had been based on a load of at least 400 kilograms, meaning three soldiers with full marching equipment plus a machine gun with a supply of ammunition. (BA)

Below: Russian Army Group South, in the autumn of 1942. The motorcyclists were constantly in action; here the driver photographs his colleague taking a nap. The two probably have a long ride behind them, and the sidecar is fully loaded. The cycle belonged-as the division emblem indicates-to the 24th Armored Division. (BA)

Right: One last skeptical look at the heavens before they move out-will they remain unseen by the Russian low-level planes? In this R 75 column an R 12 sidecar unit can be seen in second place. (BA)

Below: Motorcycle riflemen on their R 75 sidecar units on the steppes of southern Russia, early in the winter of 1942. The packed sidecars suggest a transfer. (BA)

Lower right: Italy in the autumn of 1944; paratroopers get off the R 75 and take up positions. (BA)

DKW

The DKW firm in Zschopau, Saxony, the world's greatest motorcycle manufacturer since the late Twenties, was just as interested in government contracts as any other firm. But their production was based on light two-stroke models, which did not interest the Wehrmacht. Only when medium messenger cycles were simultaneously ordered from several firms, beginning in 1938, did the army turn back to DKW and select the NZ 350 with its big one-cylinder two-stroke motor. This type, in largely production form, was delivered until into 1940, then was replaced by a special Wehrmacht version of the NZ 350/1 with a cast iron engine block and many other modifications. The small RT 125 was also delivered in small numbers as of 1939, for use as a light service vehicle at home bases. In the latter half of the war, only the RT 125 was produced instead of the 350 cc type, since it had proved to be a remarkably useful messenger cycle in not-too-heavy country, as well as being economical and available in great numbers.

Above: The DKW NZ 350 medium Wehrmacht cycle. The 11-HP two-stroke model was used by the Wehrmacht in rather large numbers as a courier cycle. In this version, with saddlebag holders and a protective plate in front of the generator cover, the DKW was delivered to the Wehrmacht from 1938 to 1943.

Right: A messenger in occupied Poland in the summer of 1941, taking a brief rest with his requisitioned civilian NZ 350. (BA)

Left: An important part of the DKW NZ 350/1 modified for the Wehrmacht was the centrifugal filter, which provided clean intake air.

Lower left: Motorcycle inspection in a training company in East Prussia, 1941. In the foreground are two DKW SB 350 from 1936 civilian production, behind them an NZ 350, as there was alternating civilian and Wehrmacht production. (BA)

Lower right: Greece, May 1941: Armored soldiers help a motorcycle messenger get his Wehrmacht NZ 350 loose. The solo machines, weighing more than 170 kilograms, were already overworked here, to say nothing of the dramatic events in Russia later. (BA)

1944

Opposite page, above and left:
The DKW NZ 350, very unsuitable for heavy cross-country use but sufficient for courier travel, was available in a modified version as of 1943. The engine block was made of cast iron rather than aluminum, a new oval side panel covered a small generator, the voltage regulator and distributor came from the 125, the centrifugal air filter went into series production, the front fender became flatter, and a small speedometer was installed. In addition, the first gear ratio was reduced (to match infantry marching speed), strengthening braces from the frame to the luggage carrier were added, and so was a side brace.

Next page: Home service with NSKK members in Hamburg, 1943; the Ardie 125 (left and center) and DKW 200 were assembled for use by an air-raid unit. (BA)

Opposite page, bottom and left:
A motorcycle whose operational uses were recognized only relatively late by the Wehrmacht was the DKW RT 125. This type had been used for light service, especially on the home front, but only as of 1943 was it discovered that its light weight of only 90 kg made for better maneuverability in heavy country. Thus the Wehrmacht version, with cast iron engine block and coil springs on the fork (previously rubber springs) was produced in great numbers until the war's end.

HH 23397
HH-3615

NSU

The Neckarsulm firm, the great rival of DKW on the German motorcycle market, had no luck with official contracts. Their sporty four-stroke one-cylinder motors were very popular among their riders, but scarcely equal to hard use with a lot of dust and dirt. Along with the 251 OSL for back-line courier service, the Wehrmacht ordered the 600 cc one-cylinder 601 OSL in 1938 and 1939 for use with sidecars. This capable machine, along with numerous requisitioned private cycles, was preferred for solo use and could, when well maintained, be the fastest courier vehicle. The emphasis in NSU production during the war was on other areas of the armaments industry.

Right and above: What has been said of the DKW 350 was also true of the NSU 251 OSL; the motorcycle was not up to heavy service in the field. Weighing barely 150 kg, and with too little ground clearance, it could be used only on paved roads. Shortages of materials also compelled NSU to use cast iron for the primary chain boxes and gearbox housings; the engine blocks of the last 1942-43 machines were also made of cast iron. Changes from the civilian version applied only to the saddlebag carrier, a protective plate for the motor on the bottom frame, and a straightened fishtail end on the muffler to hold the uniform saddlebags.

Left: Two well-equipped motorcycle messengers at the Acropolis in Athens, both riding the NSU 501 OSL, well known in civilian life as a high-performance sport cycle.

The two lower photos show a motorcycle messenger in Poland during the summer of 1941; he too rides a requisitioned civilian NSU Type 501 OSL of 1936, with open hairpin valve springs and an open lower frame. The added footboards are not from series production. It was not uncommon for the motorcycle messengers to either continue to use their own vehicles in the army or to find a good machine in the requisitioned-vehicle parks if they had the chance. (BA)

Below: The renowned motorcycle racers of the Thirties were not used as motorcycle messengers in the war, but when they made service trips, they were happy to use a motorcycle. Here one sees the DKW works driver Ewald Kluge in the saddle of an NSU 601 OSL; beside him in the sidecar is NSU works driver Heiner Fleischmann.

Lower right: The two work to get their sidecar unit going again. It is an NSU 601 OSL, the only one-cylinder cycle that ranked in the category of heavy Wehrmacht cycles, though it too was not up to hard cross-country sidecar service. This version was also modified in several ways for Wehrmacht use; as was the 250 cc NSU, it had cast iron motor parts, and the exhaust and air filter were changed. The 600 also had its saddle springs replaced by a tension spring and a large tank cover added for canister filling. (BA)

Left: The famous NSU halftrack cycle, despite its name, was not ranked among the Wehrmacht motorcycles; it was classified as Sd. Kfz. 2 in the category of halftrack towing tractors.

Left: A 1936 NSU 501 OSL with a Steib sidecar, likewise requisitioned from private ownership and in Luftwaffe service. Whether the open valve system could last long in the desert sands of North Africa is questionable. (BA)

Triumph

The Triumph-Werke of Nürnberg ranked among the big German motorcycle manufacturers in the Thirties, and naturally it was wished that their motorcycles be put to military use too, though this succeeded only in part, as the Army Weapons Office preferred the 350 cc DKW to the corresponding Triumph models when ordering medium cycles. But with their new 1939 model, the double-piston, rotary-valve two-stroke BD 250, they finally attracted a Wehrmacht contract. This motorcycle was very useful as a light messenger cycle, but its complicated technology stood in the way of its widespread use. A large number of Triumph motorcycles, produced for a long time though in small numbers, went to the Luftwaffe.

Above: A Triumph S 350 of 1936-37, with camouflage paint. This 11.5 HP two-stroke type was never delivered to the government, rather the machine in the photograph was a requisitioned vehicle.

Right: Two Triumphs and a BMW R 35 at a town command post in France. (BA)

Left: The Triumph S 350 again, seen from the drive side; for Wehrmacht service it simply had a saddlebag holder added, and the entire machine was repainted.

Lower left: Here two Triumphs stationed in France are taken out of their garage, and one can recognize the different types, with the S 350 at left. The other machine is the successor type B 350, with block motor, from 1938-39, likewise not ordered by the Wehrmacht. (BA)

Below: In front is a Triumph S 350, behind it a Zündapp K 500.

Right and below: This is the only Triumph motorcycle that was contracted for by the Wehrmacht, the BD 250/1. The double-piston two-cycle machine first went into production in 1939 and had to be modified for army service a year later. The carburetor of the rotary-valve motor was well protected under the right housing cover, but the air filter had to be moved higher. The tool formerly kept in its storage place in the oil tank now found a new home in a separate container atop the tank. Naturally, saddlebag holders and a motor-protection plate were also added here. The very powerful Triumph was very popular because of its good reliability at low engine speeds, but it was not suitable for cross-country use and also required too much maintenance for hard war service, though for the first time it had separate lubrication with an oil pump, while all other contemporary two-stroke machines got by with oil mixed into the fuel.

Left: The soldier poses on a Triumph BD 250/1 for a picture to send home.

Lower left: An advance troop of paratroopers in Tunis, North Africa, in 1942-43; at left is a Triumph BD 250/1, in the middle a BMW R 71, at right a Zündapp KS 750 sidecar unit, with an older unit in the background. (BA)

Below: A detailed view of the Triumph BD 250/1 powerplant. The aluminum cylinder is equipped with a cast liner and shows the so-called hedgehog ribbing that provided good cooling, which was important for the pistons running close beside each other in this double-piston two-stroke machine. The lever behind the brake pedal made the motor idle when stepped on.

Viktoria

This firm, likewise located in Nürnberg, had already delivered sidecar machines to the army at the end of the Twenties. In the Thirties, though, there were problems with their new models. That changed decisively with the KR 35 SN, a very sporty four-stroke one-cylinder type-the motor, incidentally, was made by Horex-Columbus. This motorcycle became the best solo machine in Wehrmacht service, with more than 12,000 of the "Engineer" (type designation of the military-version KR 35 WH) ordered by 1945.

Above and right: Although they were built in large numbers, the Viktoria KR 35 WH "Engineer" was soon forgotten. According to its data (only 145 kg, but 18 HP) it may well have been the Wehrmacht's best solo machine, with only small modifications to the civilian version (doubled footrest eyes, deeper-mounted muffler, and braces to the luggage carrier).

Upper right: A rare action photo of the Victoria (Russia, 1941). (BA)

Zündapp

Zündapp too was located in the motorcycle metropolis of Nürnberg during the war. To equip the new motorcycle units of the army, Zündapp was given the first contract in 1934, for solo and sidecar machines of Type K 500 as well as heavy sidecar units of the four-cylinder K 800. These models, scarcely modified from civilian production, were put into service in great numbers until 1937-38, including 4962 of the powerful four-cylinder model alone. The 500 cc machine, though, was slightly inferior to the BMW R 12, and so from 1938 on the KS 600, with its overhead-cam motor, was delivered to the units as a replacement and became the best sidecar-unit motorcycle until the very heavy cross-country types appeared. The pressed-steel Zündapp frame and relatively simple parallelogram front fork also turned out to be surprisingly stable, even in hard cross-country service with full loads. A light courier machine was also delivered to the Wehrmacht, the DB 200, the firm's most popular civilian model, with a 7 HP two-cycle motor. It soon wore out in wartime service, though. Since Zündapp wanted to hold an advantage over BMW, they began to design a specially-built military motorcycle in 1937-38. The result, though, on account of numerous requirements imposed by the Army Weapons Office, appeared only much later in the form of the KS 750. This cycle with powered sidecar, finally developed in cooperation with BMW, was the best cross-country vehicle of World War II, but the great expense of manufacturing and maintenance prevented more widespread use, and in addition, by the time production began in 1941-42, the tasks assigned to the motorcycle service had changed. Still in all, by the beginning of 1945, 18,286 KS 750 units had been built.

On the opposite page, the largest-displacement motorcycle of the Wehrmacht can be seen, the Zündapp K 800 W. With its side-valve four-cylinder opposed motor (22 HP), the solo cycle itself weighed a massive 215 kilograms. This machine, used mainly as a sidecar unit, was very popular among the troops despite its obvious cross-country disadvantages, for it could provide its bullish power, often urgently needed, even at the lowest engine speeds. Major problems with the cooling of the rear cylinders occurred on long column marches.

Below: The K 800 also saw service with Chiang Kai-Shek's forces in China.

Right and lower right: The major part of the machines delivered to the army by Zündapp from 1934 to 1938 was the K 500; it was seen as an alternative to the BMW R 12, but its displacement of only 250 cc made it inferior. These machines, available in great numbers, were rarely used by motorcycle rifle units, but the KS 600, available from 1937 on, was often seen in back-line service as a communication vehicle, naturally usually with a sidecar.

Left: A four-cylinder Zündapp in the 1941 Balkan campaign; the rough road was almost the limit of what this machine could handle with a full load. The pressed-steel frame, the fork with its joints in particular, and also the steering bearing, were worn out very quickly.

Above: A motorcycle rifle company of the 12th Armored Division in Russia during the summer of 1941. The Zündapp KS 600 was used here without exception. (BA)

Right: Spectacular photos such as these were used to create the myths of the German motorcycle soldiers. Here one sees training on the dreaded sand hill. But it was precisely this tough training and drill in learning driving techniques that always proved valuable in war service. Only thus was it possible to fulfill most of the assigned tasks with the actually scarcely suitable machines with which the army was originally supplied. One cannot say too much of the sometimes superhuman achievements of the motorcyclists. And so those involved really earned their good reputation.

Opposite page:
A big step forward from the K 500 W was made with the KS 600 W. The 28 HP overhead-valve powerplant was nominally the most powerful Wehrmacht motorcycle motor and gave the motorcycle riflemen considerably better service than they had previously. This Zündapp was delivered until mid-1941 and was much more highly regarded by many riders than, for example, the BMW R 12.

Right: A Zündapp motorcycle rifle column; the corporal at the front is driving a K 800

Below: This is a typical picture of a muddy Russian winter; the Zündapp KS 600 W has already lost its front fender, and the sidecar passenger can do nothing but put his weight on the spinning rear wheel.

Opposite page:
Here as they advance into the Balkans in the spring of 1941, even the motorcycle riders are stuck in the heavy traffic of the supply trains.

The pictures on this page show that Colossus of a motorcycle, the extra-heavy Zündapp KS 750 sidecar motorcycle, the first cycle developed in Germany purely for military use. As of April 1940, this project was developed in close cooperation with BMW, which also led to a certain amount of uniformity. But it was basically a matter of the BMW firm adopting the Zündapp differential with wheel-pressure-dependent torque distribution and locking, as well as the hydraulic brakes on the rear and sidecar wheels. In the massive-looking engine block, all subsidiary parts were safely enclosed, and the cylinders of the opposed motor were even raised ten degrees to improve ground clearance. The Zündapp, as opposed to the BMW R 75, had a welded frame of profiled pressed steel and a parallelogram fork, the latter being quite superior to the BMW telescopic fork though much more complex and demanding in terms of maintenance. Which of the two sidecar machines with powered sidecar was actually better has not been decided to this day, despite vigorous discussions among the soldiers who used them.

Here the great ground clearance of the Zündapp KS 750 unit can be seen, measuring 290 mm under the sidecar, and the wading ability thus amounted to a splendid 425 mm. The almost incomparable cross-country usefulness and handiness of the KS 750 and BMW R 75 cost much in production expenses, a price twice as high as that of a VW "bucket car". Yet from 1941 to 1945 some 35,000 of them were built.

Right: There were really moments when it was quite risky to get ahead, even for the Zündapp KS 750, for a skid in the mountains with its wheel pointed downward was very dangerous indeed. But as this was a test ride, planks of the proper strength were on hand.

Below: Two paratroopers underway in southern Italy on a KS 750. These machines were extremely popular among all the troops, and so almost every soldier tried to get at least one chance to drive one. The two field policemen would certainly like to change places with them. (BA)

Technical data on the motorcycles delivered to the German Wehrmacht

	Light motorcycles				*Medium motorcycles*		
Make and Type	**DKW RT 125**	**NSU 251 OSL**	**Triumph BD 250/1**	**Zündapp DB 200**	**BMW R 4**	**BMW R 35**	**DKW NZ 350**
Motor	2 stroke, 1 cylinder	4 stroke, 1 cylinder	2 stroke, 1 cylinder	2 stroke, 1 cylinder	4 stroke, 1 cylinder	4 stroke, 1 cylinder	2 stroke, 1 cylinder
Bore/stroke	52 x 58 mm	64 x 75 mm	45 x 78 mm (x 2--double piston)	60 x 70 mm	78 x 84 mm	72 x 84 mm	72 x 85 mm
Displacement	123 cc	242 cc	248 cc	196 cc	398 cc	340 cc	346 cc
HP at RPM	4.75 at 4800	10.5 at 5000	12 at 3800	7 at 3950	12 at 3500	14 at 4500	11.5 at 4000
Compression	6 : 1	6.8 : 1	5.5 : 1	6.1 : 1	5.7 : 1	6 : 1	5.7 : 1
Carburetor	Amal, Bing, Graetzin 16 mm	Amal, Bing, Graetzin 20 mm	Bing 26 mm	Bing 20 mm	Sum 3-jet	Sum 22 mm	Amal, Bing, Graetzin 24 mm
Valves	Slit	OHV	Rotary	Slit	OHV	OHV	Slit
Drive	Chain	Chain	Chain	Chain	Cardan	Cardan	Chain
Shift	3-speed foot	4-speed foot	4-speed foot	3-speed hand	4-speed hand	4-speed hand	4-speed foot
Frame	Tube	Tube	Tube	Tube	Pressed steel	Pressed steel	Pressed steel
Front fork	Parallelogram	Parallelogram	Parallelogram	Parallelogram	Leaf-spring	Telescopic	Parallelogram
Wheelbase	1230 mm	1285 mm	1320 mm	1300 mm	1320 mm	1300 mm	1355 mm
Dry weight	68 kg (aluminum block)	136 kg (aluminum block)	140 kg	105 kg	137 kg	150 kg	145 kg (aluminum block)
Fuel capacity	9 liters	11 liters	11.3 liters	12 liters	12 liters	12 liters	14 liters
Top speed	75 kph	95 kph	105 kph	85 kph	100 kph	100 kph	105 kph
Years built	1939-1945	1938-1942	1939-1943	1935-1940	1932-1936	1937-1940	1938-1944

Victoria KR 35 WH	*Heavy motorcycles* BMW R 12	NSU 601 OSL	Zündapp K 500 W	Zündapp K 800 W	Zündapp KS 600 W	*Extra-heavy motorcycles* BMW R 75	Zündapp KS 750
4 stroke, 1 cylinder	4 stroke, 2 cylinder (opposed)	4 stroke, 1 cylinder	4 stroke, 2 cylinder (opposed)	4 stroke, 4 cylinder (opposed)	4 stroke, 2 cylinder (opposed)	4 stroke, 2 cylinder (opposed)	4 stroke, 2 cylinder (opposed)
69 x 91.5 mm	78 x 78 mm	85 x 99 mm	69 x 66.6 mm	62 x 66 mm	75 x 67.6 mm	78 x 78 mm	75 x 85 mm
342 cc	745 cc	562 cc	498 cc	791 cc	587 cc	745 cc	751 cc
18 at 5000	18 at 3400	24 at 5000	16 at 4800	22 at 4300	28 at 4800	26 at 4400	26 at 4000
6 : 1	5.2 : 1	6 : 1	5.8 : 1	5.8 : 1	6.5 : 1	5.8 : 1	6.2 : 1
Amal 25 mm	Sum 3-jet	Amal 27 mm	Amal, Bing 22 mm	Amal 18 mm	Amal 25.4 mm	2 Graetzin 24 mm	Solex 30 mm
OHV	SV	OHV	SV	SV	OHV	OHV	OHV
Chain	Cardan	Chain	Cardan	Cardan	Cardan	Cardan	Cardan
4-speed foot	4-speed hand	4-speed foot	4-speed hand	4-speed hand	4-speed foot and hand	4-speed foot, reverse, and cross-country gears by hand lever	4-speed foot, reverse, and cross-country gears by hand lever
Tube	Pressed steel	Tube	Pressed steel	Pressed steel	Pressed steel	Tube	Pressed steel
Parallelogram	Telescopic	Parallelogram	Parallelogram	Parallelogram	Parallelogram	Tube	Parallelogram
1420 mm	1380 mm	1460 mm	1390 mm	1405 mm	1390 mm	1444 mm	1410 mm
145 kg	185 kg	185 kg	188 kg	210 kg	205 kg	420 kg (unit)	400 kg (unit)
13 liters	14 liters	13.5 liters	12.5 liters	12.5 liters	15 liters	24 liters	23 liters
115 kph	110 kph (solo)	130 kph (solo)	105 kph (solo)	125 kph (solo)	135 kph (solo)	92 kph (unit)	95 kph (unit)
1938-1945	1935-1941	1938-1942	1934-1938	1934-1938	1938-1941	1941-1944	1941-1945

ALSO FROM SCHIFFER MILITARY